Morsels of Love

A Book of Poetry and Short Form

Also by Carmen Micsa

Change Your Grip on Life Through Tennis!
A Player's Physical, Mental, Technical, &
Nutritional Guide for Improving Your Game

The PR – The Poetics of Running
A Book of Poetry in Motion

Morsels of Love

A Book of Poetry and Short Form

Carmen Micsa

Wistful Press
CARMICHAEL, CA

Copyright © 2021 by **Carmen Micsa**

All rights reserved. No part of this publication may be reproduced, distributed or transmitted in any form or by any means, without prior written permission.

Carmen Micsa/Wistful Press
8037 Fair Oaks Blvd., Suite 101
Carmichael, CA 95608
www.carmenmicsabooks.com

Book layout © 2021 BookDesignTemplates.com
Cover art by Carmen Micsa
Cover design by Heather Dunmoyer
Book formatting by Jenni Wiltz

Morsels of Love – A Book of Poetry and Short Form — 1st ed.
ISBN 978-0-998-3097-3-6 (paperback)
ISBN 978-0-9983097-4-3 (eBook)

Dedication

For my husband Catalin Micsa and our sweet children Alex and Sophia, as well as my father Danut Gramatic, who was a great poet with a unique sensibility to the world around him. And last, but not least, a special dedication to my wonderful friend Deirdre Fitzpatrick, KCRA news morning anchor and the host of my favorite podcast Dying to Ask, who inspired me to start writing on Medium, where I published many poems and short form pieces collected here in this book together with some new writing.

Contents

Uncommon Poetic Forms

The Daughter of Time and the Fisherman	15
Buddha's Five Teachings	19
If Fall Leaves Could Talk	23
Slivers of Gold at Sunrise	25
The Golden River	27
Squinting at the Sun	29
That Orange Orb	31
Dancing Trees	33
A Rainy California Day	35
The Lull Before the Storm	37
The Arrival of Autumn	39
Six Feet Away	41
Afternoon Tea in London	43
A Splash of Ruby	45
Last Phone Call With My Dad	47

Chewing Gum	51
Wistful Wisps	53
Soul Search	55
Dragons in the Sky	59
I Have Waited 48 Years to Eat Huckleberry Pie for the First Time — It Was So Worth It	61

Common Poetic Forms

Autumn Bandages	65
The Touch of an Aspen Tree	69
Impermanence	73
Poetry in Motion	75
Views	79
The Hawk	81
Is the Lone Cypress Really Lonely?	83
Love Unlocked	87
Listening	89
Sunset Promenade During the Pandemic	91

If Only Magnolias	95
The Song of the Wind	97
The London Selfie Queen	101
Watching the Autumn Sunset With My Daughter	105
Turning Pages	109

Short Forms

Cooking With My Dad	113
Crossword Puzzles With My Aunt	117
What's Up With All These Hills?	121
Killer Abs	125
You're Such a Garden Gnome!	129
I Am the Beast	133
Le Pain Quotidien	137
Raving Ravens	141
The Illusion of an Allusion	145
A Post Halloween Bloody Story	149
A Sad Spider Story	153

Slow and Strong Like a Sloth	157
Coyote — Trickster and Teacher	161
The Sacred Acrobats	165
Reading The Four Winds on This Windy Day	169
In the Fall I Fall For Persimmons	173
The Good Life	177
Break a Leg	181
The Enchanted Forest	185
The Painted Rocks	189
Mood Lifting? Head to the Grocery Store!	193
Light as a Feather	197
Liver Anyone?	201
Where Are the Snickerdoodles?	205
Plum Dumplings and Dracula	209
Acknowledgments	211
About the Author	213

Uncommon Poetic Forms

Somonka, Haiku, Tanka, and Etheree

Photo by Neil Mark Thomas on Unsplash

The Daughter of Time and the Fisherman

A somonka

Soon after you left
us — tired of sullen sails
my dear father
you will cast your fishing line
with joy in Heavenly lakes.

When you cried for me
I dared into your dreams
peeling sacred seams
my dear daughter of TIME
for you to never worry.

This somonka is written in response to *Literary Impulse's* prompt for the month of August, "Uncommon Poetic Forms." And this is how I fell in love with the somonka, writing quite a few after I first wrote this one. Thank you, *Literary Impulse* for the poetic impulse.

The somonka is basically two tankas (5–7–5–7–7 syllable format) written as two love letters to each other (one tanka per love letter). This form usually demands two authors, but it is possible to have a poet take on two personas.

*Photo taken by Carmen Micsa in
The Japanese Tea Garden in San Francisco*

Buddha's Five Teachings

A somonka

Running is my joy
getting in touch with the world
one step at a time
a brief breath of lingering
life—being here in the now.

There is suffering.
Truth comes to us through seeing
not from rejecting
the right view that our lives are
not frozen, but flexible.

The somonka is basically two tankas (5–7–5–7–7 syllable format) written as two love letters to each other (one tanka per love letter). This form usually demands two authors, but it is possible to have a poet take on two personas.

This peaceful statue of Buddha in the Japanese Tea Garden has inspired me to write this somonka, as a loving and kind conversation with Buddha. I also read and found inspiration in *Buddhism Plain and Simple* by Steve Hagen.

Wishing you "to be a light unto yourself," as Buddha said.

Photo taken by Carmen Micsa

If Fall Leaves Could Talk

A somonka

If fall leaves could talk
they would choose to paint pictures
on the permanent
plaque of time in heavy brush
strokes — ruby, yellow, and gold.

If I chose to talk
to fall leaves and sink myself
in piles of rustling
ruby seasonal beauty
I would turn life into gold.

Photo taken by Carmen Micsa during her 10-mile run

Slivers of Gold at Sunrise

Haiku

Slivers of stillness
turn the river into gold
the geese swim and float.

Photo taken by Rob Schmidt during our run

The Golden River

The sun splayed gold at sunrise - haiku

Yet burnished with gold
the silence of the river
transcends across town.

This haiku was inspired by another California sunrise during my 17-mile long run in preparation for London marathon that I ran on October 3rd. The gold pouring down the river, so to speak, make me think of The Yellow River in China, which is named that way, because of its yellow-brown color. When the river overflows, it leaves a yellow residue behind. What a spectacle!

Photo by Melissa Askew on Unsplash

Squinting at the Sun

Sharpen your eyes - haiku

Observe with clear eyes
thoughts and feelings more pronounced
the kind sun smiling.

My haiku was inspired by reading *Klara and the Sun* by Kazuo Ishiguro. We can all sharpen our observation skills if we do some "good looking," as my daughter used to tell me when she was little.

Photo by Carmen Micsa taken during her run with friends on July 15th, 2021

That Orange Orb

*Running early in the morning to see
a glorious sunrise is rewarding - haiku*

Sliver of sunrise

the sun spray-paints the still trail

the jackrabbit leaps.

Photo taken by Carmen Micsa, Jensen Botanical Gardens

Dancing Trees

A love romance - haiku

Leaning limbs linger
and welcome today's blue skies
lovers' footprints seen.

Photo by Hannah Domsic on Unsplash

A Rainy California Day

It rarely rains this hard in October - a haiku

Rain splinters the sky
Puddles of water plunge drought
I read a novel.

Photo taken by Carmen Micsa at the start of a long run

The Lull Before the Storm

A haiku

The sky — an old man's
furrowed brow bending darkness
the storm's seeping through.

Photo by Lucas Albuquerque on Unsplash

The Arrival of Autumn

And the Halloween ghosts – a haiku

Cool crisp crinkle air
chilling the bones of steamy
summer roaming ghosts.

Photo taken by Carmen Micsa, Ancil Hoffman Park

Six Feet Away

Social distancing at the end of summer – a haiku

The evening sun splayed
reddish reflections draped in
daily solitude.

This haiku was inspired by a sunset walk with my husband. The heron and the egret kept their social distancing — not big risk takers...

Photo taken by Carmen Micsa in London, 2021

Afternoon Tea in London

Steeped in tea and tradition – a haiku

London — a place steeped
in history and glory
I savor afternoon tea.

Photo taken by Carmen Micsa, Ancil Hoffman Park

A Splash of Ruby

Autumn splendor – a tanka

Autumn splendor is
not subtle when all the leaves
splash ruby across
the cerulean serene
sky stitched in a golden frame.

A form of waka, Japanese song or verse, tanka translates as "short song," and is better known in its five-line, 5/7/5/7/7 syllable count form.

Photo by Darren Lawrence on Unsplash

Last Phone Call With My Dad

I thought I heard him for a second – a tanka

For one brief second
my dad picked up the phone, but
then I heard a pause.
I dialed again thinking
that the living shall prevail.

This tanka is based on a true story of my last phone call ever with my dear father, who died of a sudden heart attack at the age of 53. He died alone. I am not sure if my dad was trying to get to the phone, or if it was just my imagination, or a poor phone connection. I kept calling him for a few days in a row, thinking that he was out of town, but then my mom called to tell me that the neighbors found my father dead in his apartment.

It hurts so much not to know what happened in these last moments and his last breath on this planet, but from my dreams of him and his bright smiles, I know that my father is happy — constantly watching over me.

Smiling can never disappear from our memory, but it can certainly brighten up the sullenest skies and souls.

My father is at peace, and so am I.

Photo by Karina Miranda on Unsplash

Chewing Gum

A tanka

A pink elastic
a somersault sweet saga
I feel scholastic
listening to my teachers
and chewing flexible thoughts.

As a child, I have always liked to chew gum, especially pink one, for I thought it was more flavorful and way cooler. As an adult, I still love gum, but I look for quality brands and the dentist recommended one for improving gum health and reducing cavities. Needless to say, my chewing gum is rarely pink nowadays.

Colorful chewing gums are cool, but not healthy.

Chew on this!

Photo taken by Bryn Mumma during our 20-mile run

Wistful Wisps

A tanka

Figments of thin fog
whispering wistful wisps crossed
the bike trail — a tale
of midsummer night's dreams full
of hope for humanity.

I have run thousands of miles on the American River Parkway in the last six years since I became a runner, and yet, I can always find indelible threads of inspiration and imagination.

Many thanks to my wonderful friend Bryn, who ran 20 miles with me today, and took this great picture, while we both admired the wisps of fog. She inspired me to write this tanka, which is a thirty-one-syllable poem, traditionally written in a single unbroken line.

*Photo taken by the author during her
10-mile run by the American River*

Soul Search

Seeking solitude- an etheree

Perched
above
the river
seeking signs of
fish swimming downstream
hoisted above world's woes
the white egret transports the
souls of the departed people
to Heaven in a state of balance,
harmony, good fortune, and zeal for life.

I believe that my father has come back to this life as an egret, which is why I never fail to take egret pictures during my walking, running, and biking in nature. Not only was my father a great fisherman, but he also had a keen eye, peering inside minuscule watch mechanisms that he used to repair.

The poetry form etheree consists of 10 lines of 1, 2, 3, 4, 5, 6, 7, 8, 9, 10 syllables. Etheree can also be reversed and written 10, 9, 8, 7, 6, 5, 4, 3, 2, 1.

Photo taken by Carmen Micsa during her 20-mile run

Dragons in the Sky

Playing tag — an etheree

When
dragons
play tag and
spit flamboyant
flames of fire in
the sky — hurling orange
and red torches — a fiery,
fierce battle begins to signal
that mankind is still masked on this day
of Halloween full of witches flying.

Photo taken by the author in White Fish, Montana

I Have Waited 48 Years to Eat Huckleberry Pie for the First Time — It Was So Worth It

An etheree

The
first time
I ate pie
oozing with sweet
Montana berries
my taste buds burst in
huckleberry hypnosis
of my tongue teaching the mind to
taste and toast to all life's lyrical
luscious flavors — scintillating my soul.

Common Poetic Forms

Photo taken by Carmen Micsa

Autumn Bandages

Mending mankind

Stricken with grief
levitating leaves
coalesce in their free fall
and turn into autumn bandages
mending mankind of every kind.

Stickers of stolen joy
peeled from their luscious lives
fall leaves kiss the damp ground
after a sudden storm
mending mankind of every kind.

Saddled with sorrow
for an unknown tomorrow
fall leaves stick together
in a mosaic of color
mending mankind of every kind.

Autumn bandages
stricken with solitude
stickers of renewed joy
saddled with daunting dreams
mending mankind of every kind.

**Mending mankind of every kind
with stickers of renewed joy**

This poem was inspired by my five-mile run around my neighborhood the day after a 100-year storm that hit Sacramento hard and beat the record set in 1880, which was 5.28 inches vs. this year's 5.44 inches. The 100-year storm has a one percent chance of occurring in any given year.

As I ran by these vibrant leaves glued to the ground like a wig, I snapped a picture. That's how this poem of healing was born with the reminder that we have the ability to transform our lives into stickers of renewed joy after each inner or outer storm if we coalesce together for the greater good.

Photo taken by Carmen Micsa in Lake Tahoe, CA

The Touch of an Aspen Tree

A tactile experience

On a warmer than usual October day
my husband and I drove to Lake Tahoe,
where the lake inked the shores
with its perfect blue waters,
and groves of aspen trees
with golden coin-shaped leaves
chattered in the light wind.
The views delighted us at every turn in the road
and pulled us away from the lake, but got us
closer to the aspen trees that shielded us
from the world's follies and shattered dreams,
since the word aspen comes from the Greek
"aspis," which means shield.

"We need to walk through the aspen grove,"
I said with more excitement than when
I first saw the Statue of Liberty.

We stopped on the side of the road
across from the lake
and noticed that the grove was full of people
posing with the trees and taking mindless selfies,
but yet, no one touched the bark.
"I need to talk to the aspens," I told my husband,
while touching the smooth, white bark
that felt as soft as my grandmother's hand,
as delicate as a rose petal,
as thin as silk,
as warm as a pair of mittens
hugging the hands on a cold winter night,
as tender as a mother holding her child
for the first time,
as loving as the first hand holding
with your lover,
and as healing as a hot cup of tea
made from the smooth, white bark
of an aspen tree.

Photo taken by Carmen Micsa in Ancil Hoffman Park, her "slice of Paradise"

Impermanence

The shiny shadows of the
tangerine and lemon-hued leaves
bent towards the river
in an eternal bow
that climaxed in an impassioned,
but impermanent kiss of the still water below.

Photo taken by my awesome friend Kristie Gong.
Folsom Lake, 2021

Poetry in Motion

Writing on the run is more fun

When I first became a runner
I discovered dancing words
that floated freely in my mind
and filled my soul with serenity.

When I first became a poet
I didn't need a pen, my laptop, or my office
to type away life's illusions and allusions.
All I needed were my running shoes
to take me outdoors in nature
where words, images, and ideas
were so easy to capture.

When I first started to pile up
my poems — heaps of hope
I would run in nature
where my thoughts were nurtured.

When I first published my poetry book
The PR — The Poetics of Running —
A Book of Poetry in Motion
during the pandemic in 2020
I collected many nature's narratives
and turned them into serendipitous stanzas.

I run, therefore I write.

Photo taken by Carmen Micsa, Folsom Lake

Views

Poem dedicated to my amazing friend Deirdre Fitzpatrick, KCRA news anchor and host of my favorite podcast Dying to Ask

During a spring trail run around Folsom Lake,
I relished a rapturous sunrise
that splayed golden stretch streaks
over a retreating and regressing lake.
I snapped a few splendid shots
and felt like a victorious viewer
who had to share her vibrant views.

I texted my wonderful friend Deirdre.
"Gorgeous," she texted right back,
and shared her hi-tech views
of the KCRA news TV studio.
"I love the bright lights and your inner view
into people's hearts and souls,
which is hard to beat, repeat, or tweet."
My friend replied: "You're so sweet."

Photo taken by the author on American River Parkway

The Hawk

Dedicated to Mrs. Deb Mumma

Perched on the top branches of a tree
on the American River Parkway
the hawk can see eight times better than humans,
can grasp messages from the Great Spirit,
can dive to capture its prey at 150 mph,
and can recognize people's faces.
Meanwhile, as I take the picture
of this majestic hawk during my run,
I acquiesce that although humans cannot match
the superpowers of the hawk,
we can at least hang on tight
to the branches of life
while enjoying the best views
with increased attention, optimism,
strength, courage, and spiritual awareness
despite our poor eyesight.

Photo by Carmen Micsa during a fun e-bike tour of Carmel's 17-mile drive together with my wonderful friend Andrea, Carmel, CA

Is the Lone Cypress Really Lonely?

Official symbol of Pebble Beach and one of the most photographed trees in North America

Standing on a granite hillside
supported by steel cables
the lone cypress — a twisted tree
looks lonely in its lankiness
maybe still mourning
the loss of its limbs in the 2019 storm.

Overlooking the Pacific Ocean
the lone cypress has lived and loved life
for the last 250 years,
has generated its own gravitas,
has bartered and battled with time
in an attempt to defend its loneliness
even when being photographed
ad infinitum by tourists like me
with one question deeply rooted in our minds:

Is the lone cypress really lonely?
Or are we trying to cover our own loneliness
and bury it deep inside our sinuous souls?

Photo taken by the author in Twin Falls, ID

Love Unlocked

Unlocking us through love

The sign on the side of I-80 East freeway
"Lock your love in Lovelock,"
conjured up locks, keys, prisons,
detention, dejection, and lack of bliss,
when in reality the shackles of love -
handcuffs of the heart -
need to be unleashed and unhinged
into the open lane of love,
where lovers can unlock
love's deepest layers of
touch, tenderness, and togetherness
with no keys, or tools other than
their whispering hearts and souls.

Photo taken by the author during her early morning run through Ancil Hoffman Park

Listening

Maybe having longer ears would help us listen better

Running at sunrise with serenity
somersaults my soul and
unspools the tangles of my being
to match my stride on the soft trails.

Running at sunrise with joy
brings me closer to nature
and all the marvelous creatures
that hop around the bristle brush.

Running at sunrise with hope
I see the jackrabbits' lean and long ears
and, as I dust off my eyes, I realize
that I must dust off my ears, too.

Photo taken by Carmen Micsa at Ancil Hoffman Park

Sunset Promenade During the Pandemic

Poem dedicated to my dear father Dan Gramatic, who's watching over me from Heaven

On a warm spring evening
I went on a short walk
with no earbuds
other than my ears
tuning in to nature's mix of
soft murmurs, rustles, and croaking sounds
that reminded me of my childhood
back in Romania
when I used to go to my grandparents' house
with my dad
passing by a small and smelly swamp
full of boisterous croaking frogs
that jumped and bounced all over the sidewalk.

My dad used to tell me:
"Don't be scared of the frogs.

They are just welcoming you
with a strident serenade."
Now as an adult, remembering
my father's wise and comforting words,
I delve in deeper into every croak
and become one with nature's serenade
on this warm spring evening promenade.

Photo taken by Carmen Micsa, Carmichael, CA

If Only Magnolias

If only we figured out
how to turn our frowns
into smiles as wide as magnolias.
If only our hearts and souls
were as opened as bloomed magnolias
in early spring.

If only magnolias,
white petals of longevity,
which existed since the beginning of times,
If only magnolias
pink petals of perseverance

If only magnolias...

Photo by Robin van der Ploeg on Unsplash

The Song of the Wind

Murmuring stories

What does the wind say?
It murmurs songs and stories
of sadness and melancholy.
It also sings songs of suffering,
of longing and unrequited love,
as it whips and whirls around.

What else does the wind say?
It roars around town,
with a swivel and pivot
blowing and leaving leaves
breathless — while they
bind and stick
to the wet and weeping ground.

It is the song of the wind
singing a soggy story
on a wild, wet October California day.

The song of the wind.
The call of the wild.

Photo by Alexandru Zdrobău on Unsplash

The London Selfie Queen

Different angles and poses

Traveling by train, subway, or tube
is as foreign to me as British bangers,
but on my recent trip to London
I sit across a young woman
with purple hair pinned underneath her beret.

I smile at the selfie queen
who, self-absorbed and self-centered,
poses, while increasing the number of selfies,
as if she were a tennis player
practicing various serves,
focused on the location, light, and length
to immortalize her perennial purple hair.

I smile at the selfie queen
who clicks away one selfie after another,
switching her iPhone from the right hand —

heavily decorated with big stone rings-
to the left one.

I smile at the selfie queen clad
in a black dress that matched
her ankle-length boots,
while she parts her hair
to the right and then the left,
with an everlasting pout.

I smile at the selfie queen
while she traces and tracks time
on the London tube.

Photo taken by Carmen Micsa

Watching the Autumn Sunset With My Daughter

Sunsets are more vivid in the fall

"Let's go and watch the sunset,"
my daughter said dashing out the door.
"I'm coming," I replied ready to
revere and revel in the resplendent
autumn colors.

Standing in the driveway with my daughter
I feel the alchemy of autumn
audaciously advance across
the sky — chariots of fire —
blend the pink and orange
into a giant celestial peach.

Watching the colors converge
at the confluence of time,
my daughter and I converse

about the evening sky
and seal our sighting with a hug.

Once back inside, I google facts
about the autumnal equinox.

After reading about the reddish autumn sky
and the rainbow lesson about the blue light
that scatters away making the red and orange
colors dance across the sky in a daring drama,
I acquiesce the autumnal adventures
that advance
towards the evening sky
in vanishing brush strokes,
while I hold this memory in my mind and heart
in the never disappearing color of love.

Photo by Jaredd Craig on Unsplash

Turning Pages

Libraries are labyrinths of pages

Turning pages plunges us
into the infinite world of books
where ideas levitate and gravitate
in and out of our lives —
where the power of knowledge
lies in the diving, delving, and devouring books.

Turning pages tethers us to immortality
giving our solitude the elegant hope
that Borges felt cheered
as the eternal traveler on life's
paths where passengers pass by
uplifted and enlightened by
the power of reading thousands of pages.

Turning pages inside and outside of a library
brings us closer to God
with the infinite knowledge that
makes us imperfect intelligent beings

finding hope and humility
in the number of books
turning page after page, after page, after page…

The Library of Babel by Jorge Luis Borges was my inspiration for this poem.

Short Forms

Photo taken by Carmen Micsa

Cooking With My Dad

My dad made the best polenta

In this 111-degree Sacramento weather, I made polenta. As I stirred it vigorously for the corn to be well-mixed, I remembered my dad, who used to get as giddy as a kid when making polenta for my mom and me.

"Look at this! Pure gold," he would point at his mushy culinary masterpiece. His blue eyes transfixed on the healthy and nutritious food he prepared for us with love almost every day.

Growing up in communist Romania, my friends and I used to call polenta "the poor people's meal," as it only required water, salt, and cornmeal to make.

More than 30 years later, on this scorching hot day, I feel the richest daughter in the world, remembering and cooking with my dad — adding some butter at the end for the creamiest and most golden polenta.

Photo by Robert Linder on Unsplash

Crossword Puzzles With My Aunt

She solves no more

My aunt and I used to devour and dive into crossword puzzles for hours. We would not stop till we finished an entire book after which we would hunt for another one.

Our favorite crosswords were the ones about literature, books, and arts.

"I know the author," I would shout with excitement.

"Great job!" my aunt would reply beaming with pride — telling me how smart I was.

Snuggled against each other, pencil in hand, answering all kinds of questions, I never thought that one day, I would need to find my way out of death's dark labyrinth.

My aunt just passed away at 90 in Romania. She is no longer solving crossword puzzles, but I already think of her.

Puzzled. Trying to solve the ultimate crossword — of death and dying — at no avail.

Photo taken by Carmen Micsa. One of the many hills in my neighborhood. Carmichael, CA

What's Up With All These Hills?

A rhetorical question about the ups and downs of life

During our 10-mile hilly bike ride, my son and I had a few hills to overcome.

As a marathon runner, I used to dread hills, but after a few years of practice, the hills and I have bonded. I now feel empowered running, or biking on a steep hill, knowing how much I will relish the view.

Standing on the edges of time at the top. Catching my breath. Breathing in the air in big gulps to satisfy my thirst of life, while my lungs and heart join in a tumultuous drum concert loud enough to wake up my ancestors.

"Mom, what's up with all these hills?" my son asked, pedaling hard."

"Nothing," I replied. They're just hills, and we conquered them.

Photo by Clem Onojeghuo on Unsplash

Killer Abs

*"Longest 10-minute of my life,"
people commented on YouTube.*

Since the pandemic started, my teenage kids and I have used YouTube for our exercise.

At first, it felt weird not to be in a studio setting, but soon it had become a convenience to have Pamela Reif, my daughter's favorite trainer, lead us into a workout.

Today, my daughter decided that we were ready for the 10-minute killer six pack ab workout. We lay on the soft carpet in her bedroom and started doing continuous crunches, bicycles, obliques until we were on the brink of exhaustion. To our surprise, the plank was the easiest and felt like rest.

"No kidding! This is a killer ab workout!" I told my daughter, breathing hard, as if the air were laden with mothballs.

"If it's hurting, it means it's working," she replied.

Photo by Dorota Dylka on Unsplash

You're Such a Garden Gnome!

My daughter tells me often

I was born to short parents — both about 5 feet tall.

As an only child, I got used to being called "the little one" by family and friends. Some were even more specific and would call me "the little girl with the pretty green eyes."

Now, as the mother to my Sophia, who is a high schooler, we're both exactly five feet tall. Sophia's got my height, although she would like to be taller like my husband and her brother, but no.

She is my little one. And I am her little one.

***

This evening, I showed Sophia the new running beanie that a good friend and real estate client knitted for me as a gift for helping her buy a house.

Sophia looked at me and gushed out:

"You're such a garden gnome, Mom!"

Photo taken by Carmen Micsa in Old Fair Oaks, CA

I Am the Beast

But not the one you think — or maybe that one!

Just as Japan has a rabbit island, so does Old Fair Oaks, CA have hundreds of chickens and wild roosters.

However, let's not get down the rabbit hole, or the chicken one, since this story is about the yearly chicken five-mile race. Runners not only race the roosters roaming the streets, but they actually have four infamous hills to climb: Grand Daddy hill, Hernia hill, the Beast, and The Last Gasp.

I ran this race for the first time and enjoyed running over hills, through rocks by the river single-track path, and on a gravel road.

As I finished the gravel section, one of the volunteers cheered on us to run strong on the Beast hill.

My response to him: "I am the beast."

Photo taken by Carmen Micsa, London

Le Pain Quotidien

A story of bread and pain

"I love pain. The right kind of pain. The one that makes you grow stronger mentally and physically." — Unknown

As I explored London and Marylebone, the chic neighborhood, where I rented a cute condo through Airbnb, I came across Le Pain Quotidien.

As a marathoner, I immediately thought of the daily pain that we sometimes experience during our heavy training, even though the name of the restaurant means "the daily bread" in French. Furthermore, the website of this chain says: "and to us, that means everything. It's much more than mere sustenance; it's a way of life," which also matches what runners think of running.

Bread's recipe: flour, water, salt, and time.

The simple joys of life don't require much, and that was one of the things I savored most about my European trip.

Photo taken by Carmen Micsa at the Tower of London, Oct. 2021

Raving Ravens

And the Ravenmaster

Jubilee, Harris, Gripp, Rocky, Erin, Poppy and Georgie are the tower ravens not Santa's reindeer.

As a first-time tourist visiting London, I purchased the London Pass and tried to do as many interesting tours and activities as possible during my recent visit.

Little did I know that I would also meet one of the seven ravens guarding the Tower so that it doesn't fall, according to legends.

Intelligent birds, who have the ability to play games and even solve problems, the ravens are taken care of by a Ravenmaster, who carefully clips their feathers and provides them with plenty of food to keep them there.

Sounds like a comfortable life, but we must keep our wings intact to move freely around the world, or we might become captive.

We must continue to fly.

Photo by Steven Weeks on Unsplash

The Illusion of an Allusion

And the delusion of the English language

The English language is nothing but a bag of semantic, syntactic, and phonetic tricks that pop up like a bunny out of the magician's hat.

Is the magician's bunny an illusion, allusion, or delusion?

I would say all, since the words share the same root, are spelled and sound quite similar, but with such different meanings.

Illusion is connected to deception and misleading, allusion to indirectness, and delusion reveals "something that is falsely believed." However, all the three words come from the Latin ludere, meaning "to play."

To sum up these three words for easy memorization:

1. illusion is the magician's misleading and deceiving image of a bunny.

2. allusion is the bunny being closest to reality.

3. delusion is the deceiving notion of a bunny, or us being the furthest from reality.

Abracadabra!

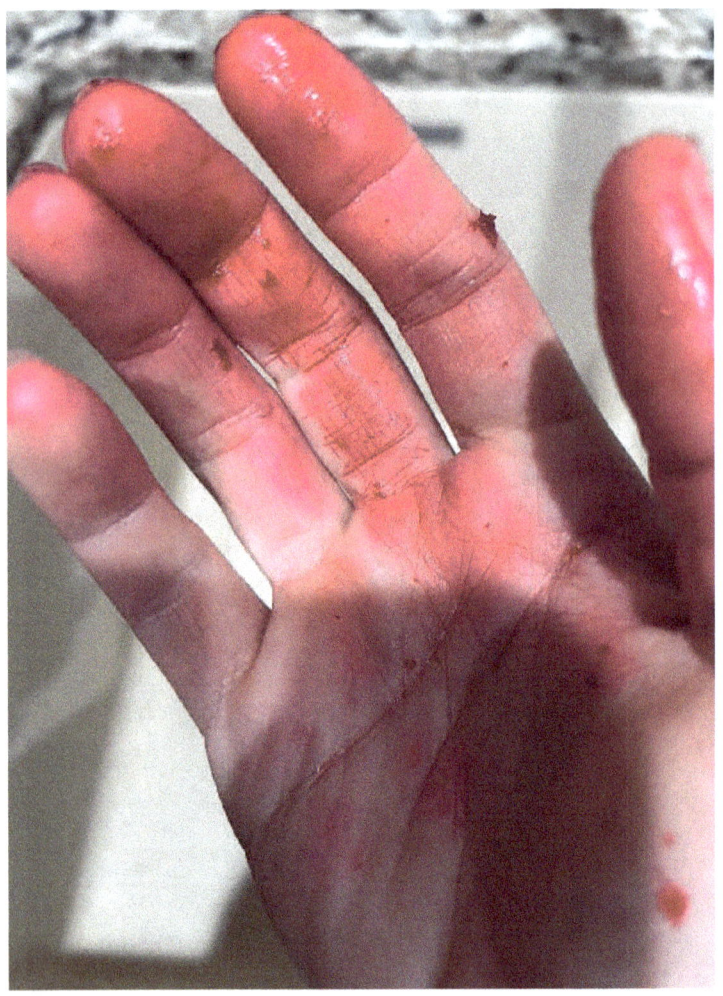

Photo taken by Carmen Micsa

A Post Halloween Bloody Story

Full of horror

"Where there is no imagination, there is no horror."
— Arthur Conan Doyle

The knife sliced and diced mixed veggies, celery, carrots, and onions on the glass cutting board with the fat, smiley chef on it. The sharp blade slashed the veggies — perfect geometric cubes of freshness.

I hummed a random tune and timed my chopping with the precision of a watchmaker. Calculating inches…Pretending to be the chef that I will never be. Glad that there was nobody around…

"Mom, I need a new backpack," my teenage son said, sauntering right behind me.

The knife slides and slips.

I turn — raising my splattered hand.

"Mom! What happened?" "Your hand is bloody! Are you OK? Did you cut yourself?"

"No, darling." "I just finished cutting some beets for my borscht soup.

"Geez, Mom!" "You scared me."

Photo by Khushbu hirpara on Unsplash

A Sad Spider Story

Fall leaves and pumpkin spices? Nope!

Among many of my nicknames, I have one that I'm not so proud of: "the spider killer."

Ever since our daughter Sophia was little, she had developed arachnophobia. She would kick and scream till I jumped into action — dashing to crash the spider and flush it down the toilet.

Just this week alone, Sophia has found at least three spiders for me to get rid of.

I didn't think much about the abundance of these creepy, crawling creatures roaming around till I read an article about the fall season being the time for male spiders to leave their webs in search of a mature female.

How valiant these spiders are! And how wonderful they are for getting rid of insects and mosquitos!

Maybe I should stop killing them and just move them to the garage.

Photo by Sophia Müller on Unsplash

Slow and Strong Like a Sloth

Sloths are three times stronger than us

When going to the movie theaters used to be a thing, the kids and I saw the commercial for a new movie Zootopia. We thought it was hilarious and wanted to see it.

Just recently, I listened to Lucy Cooke, a zoologist talk about the slothful nature of sloths on NPR. She expounded upon three main facts:

1. As energy-saving creatures, sloths move like a slow-motion ballet dancer, reminding us to savor life's moments.

2. Sloths teach us to appreciate patience over efficiency and speed.

3. Sloths hang upside down in a tree, gaining a different vantage point.

Although sloths take 30 days to digest a leaf, there is only one thing that they do swiftly: SEX.

Slow and strong like a sloth?

Photo taken by Bryn Mumma during our 12-mile run through Ancil Hoffman Park. August 14, 2021.

Coyote — Trickster and Teacher

Very few animals are as complex and controversial as the coyote

When my kids were little, I took them to a nature hike at Effie Yeaw Nature Center, or what I call "my slice of Paradise."

The naturalist, a gifted storyteller, whose stories rolled out like marbles, delighted us with a few cute animal stories. Yet, we loved the story about the trickster coyote the most for his cunning, clever, and tricky ways.

The coyote — sly and resourceful, a teacher of wisdom, has been credited with bringing the gift of fire to mankind.

The good and evil, the sacred and the profane — in the shape of my favorite animal that I am fortunate to see during my runs through parks and on the American River Parkway.

Photo by Anchor Lee on Unsplash

The Sacred Acrobats

Hummingbirds are considered messengers from the afterworld

I always call my runs magical, as I never know what I will experience — or learn from them.

Today was no exception. After our run my friend Andrea and I rested on the benches underneath a thick canopy of trees. We chatted until we noticed many hummingbirds zipping around on top of tree branches.

Our conversation shifted to these sacred acrobats, who can fly upside-down and backwards.

We tried to take their picture, but all we got was a black, blurry dot on our I-phones. Buzzing all around us — their hearts beating up to 1,200 times per minute, it's no wonder that hummingbirds have a metabolism 100 times faster than of an elephant.

"See what happens when you sit underneath trees?" I said, as we bid goodbye to our fast friends.

Photo taken by Carmen Micsa

Reading The Four Winds on This Windy Day

Soggy and rainy October day

The dry, hot California summers have been part of my life for the last 26 years since we moved to Sacramento from Romania.

Although I miss the luscious landscape of other states where summer thunderstorms dump buckets of rain and keep things green, I relish the dryness of our summer and its predictability, for it allows me run all the miles training for my marathons.

On this stormy October day, I hunker down with *The Four Winds* watching the wind whip trees and their brittle branches faster than the highest setting of the windshield wipers.

I smile at the book cover. I listen to the rain and wind converging in a stormy conversation, but I disengage.

All I need is a good book and a cup of tea to cut through life's sogginess.

Photo by Bryam Blanco on Unsplash

In the Fall I Fall For Persimmons

I eat them like an apple

Besides cool, crisp mornings, changing leaves, and shorter days, persimmons permeate my palate every single fall.

My favorite variety of persimmons are Fuyu. They're one of the oldest (more than 2,000 years ago) fruits cultivated in Asia, smaller than the Hachiya variety and less astringent. I love to eat them like apples — biting through their thick skin, but not worrying about seeds.

Not only do I relish the taste of persimmons every fall, but I am impressed with the all the vitamins and nutrients that this orange fruit packs: manganese, beta-carotene, vitamin C, and iron. Yet, betulinic acid makes the fruit even more potent due to its antiretroviral, anti-inflammatory, and potential anticancer benefits.

And this is why I love the sweet tangy taste of fall in a bowl.

Photo by Bruce Christianson on Unsplash

The Good Life

Drifting with direction

I complimented the woman next to my swim lane on her pink sun hat.

"It's called sun shades," she replied proudly. "It even has two drawstrings to adjust it on the head and under the chin," she continued.

Reclined on her water noodle, the woman in the pink hat and matching SPF-50 long-sleeve shirt drifted in her swim lane — her water shoes splashing in the pool.

I remembered the negative comment of a dad to his son about drifting in the pool with no purpose in life on the recent podcast *Presenting Hidden Brain: Unlocking Your Purpose — Chasing Life — Omny.fm*

What if our state of relaxation leads to unlocking our purpose, or just living the good life for a brief moment hidden behind sun shades and resting back on a noodle squinting at the sun?

And for the record, I did end up buying a blue sun shades hat from Amazon. What else can I say about my short swim? Well, I wrote a story, had a lovely conversation with a gregarious stranger, I experienced a new drifting appreciation of life, and bought a new hat! Isn't life grand?

Photo by Dayne Topkin on Unsplash

Break a Leg

The origin behind this phrase

I always felt uncomfortable wishing someone to break a leg, instead of wishing them good luck.

Josh Chetwynd, author of *The Book of Nice*, delves into the origin of this phrase:

1. When a woman curtsies, she bends her back leg, or she's breaking that leg.

2. Actors are considered a superstitious lot, so they would say the opposite of what they wish to avoid jinxing a performance.

3. The phrase can also be a reference to Sarah Bernhardt's exquisite acting, even after she had one of her legs amputated.

English is not the only language with peculiar expressions. For instance, the Italians wish someone good fortune by saying "in boca al lupo," which literally means "in the mouth of the wolf."

My wishes to you: "good luck," 'don't break a leg," and "don't get eaten by a wolf."

*Photo by author taken on the
American Bike Trail, Sacramento*

The Enchanted Forest

I didn't know this truly existed...

I have been a runner for six years and have run thousands of miles on the American River Parkway, which is 32 miles long, stretching from Folsom to Old Sacramento.

As I started to explore the bike trail with my runner friends, I discovered that Strava (fitness app tracking running and cycling) named one of the shady stretches of our bike trail with trees bending to greet one another and lending a listening ear "the enchanted forest."

"Wow!" "I like the name of this segment," Andrea chimed in.

"I do, too," I replied, mesmerized. "And yet looking at the trees forming a formidable canopy, I would call this section "the tunnel of love."

"I love that even more," Andrea replied, and we continued running through forests and tunnels of love.

Bewitched.

Photo taken by Carmen Micsa

The Painted Rocks

The things we see and the ones we don't

An Easter basket in the middle of summer? I blurted out after my friend Bryn spotted them in the front lawn of a house towards the end of our run.

"Painted rocks!"

The intricate, detailed design made me think of the Romanian hand-painted Easter eggs.

And just like this artist used blue, purple, green, and pink colors coalescing in the front yard art, my fellow Romanians painted the eggs in red to symbolize love and solar light, black for eternity, yellow for rich crops, green for nature, and blue to symbolize health and sunny skies.

"I'm so glad you stopped me to see this exquisite rock art," I told Bryn.

"Well, I was debating whether to stop our run, but I knew you would enjoy this," she said.

"You're a great friend," I replied.

Photo by Ginny Rose Stewart on Unsplash

Mood Lifting? Head to the Grocery Store!

Dedicated to Izzy for making my day

My son wanted chicken parmesan for dinner, so we went to Safeway to buy some Italian seasoning, bread crumbs, and Parmesan cheese.

After we parked, I saw Izzy, one of my real estate colleagues, walk fast past us. With our masks on — perfect disguise — she didn't recognize us. I said "Hi."

"Oh, my Gosh! Your son is so tall and handsome," she told me, as we reminisced about the times that I brought Alex in his car seat to our regional meetings and tours.

"And you look amazing," Izzy continued. "Your mom looks like she could be your sister." We all chuckled.

"What a compliment!" I said to Alex, as I walked into the store with a big grin.

Who knew grocery shopping could be so uplifting?

Photo by Marek Okon on Unsplash

Light as a Feather

And why I keep it on my desk

"Let's go foraging for blackberries at Ancil Hoffman Park," I told Alex and Sophia, who were about 8 and 6 at the time.

We walked/jogged about half a mile on the shaded soft trails towards the blackberry bushes. Zipper bag in hand — ready to harvest, Alex stopped suddenly to pick up a brown and white hawk feather that rested lightly and mixed in with the trail.

"We could use it as a pen," he exclaimed!

"Yeah, like we did in school," Sophia chimed in.

We rejoiced in the feather, and like any modern mom with a social media account, I snapped a picture of the kids holding the feather.

"I'll keep the feather in my office forever!"

"And don't forget to get some ink and write with it, Mom," Alex said.

Photo by Carmen Micsa.
Polenta, spinach, fried eggs, and liver. I tried to make a happy face, but it looks rather melancholic.

Liver Anyone?

Hard pass, or not?

Growing up in communist Romania, I used to eat brains, tongue, giblets, heart, and way too much liver, as organ meats were cheap.

My mom used to fry the liver with salt, pepper, and garlic. I loved it until one day when I ended up vomiting from noon to late at night.

From that day on, I avoided eating liver, as I could not forget my shooting projectile. I might have ejected my own liver, for all I could tell.

Fast forward about 37 years later - beef liver for lunch, as it nourishes my thyroid and it provides an excellent source of iron for this marathon runner.

So, yeah! I now love the liver and eat it about once a month.

Photo taken by Carmen Micsa after stocking up on Snickerdoodles at Trader Joe's.

Where Are the Snickerdoodles?

These vegan, gluten-free cookies are the most underrated at Trader Joe's.

I was at the post office heading back home when I got a phone call from Sophia, who blurted out: "Mom, where are the snickerdoodles?"

"I think Alex ate them all," she continued with panic in her voice as if announcing that there was no more water in the oceans.

"I am going to Trader Joe's now," I replied — recognizing the state of emergency.

As I drove to Trader Joe's, I realized that snacking on the Unreal brand of chocolate has been my way to handle these unreal times, and thus, buying a few boxes of the soft-baked, not too sweet, and delectable cookies for my kids was not indulging.

It was simply an act of sweet love.

Photo taken by Carmen Micsa after spending two hours making plum dumplings.

Plum Dumplings and Dracula

Plum dumplings were one of my favorite desserts growing up in Romania.

The only fruit tree we have in our yard is a plum tree that came with our property. Today I picked a big bag and decided to make plum dumplings.

Unsure of the recipe, I found one on a Romanian food and folklore blog "From Dill to Dracula."

As always, I adapted the recipe, used gluten-free flour, and added a little bit of cold water to the composition, which made the dumplings melt into our mouths like snowflakes on a warmer winter day.

My husband asked me if I remembered what I did this time, as they came out much better than before.

I nodded, thinking of the blog's name: "It's not garlic. It's the flour and the water."

Acknowledgments

A million thanks to the following who have shaped this book and have helped me over the years become the writer/poet I am today: Jenni Wiltz, my Sac State classmate, friend, and brilliant writer, who has helped me with all the publishing and formatting process of this book and my other two books, Doug Rice, my most inspiring creative writing professor and acclaimed author, Sheree Meyer, the Chair of the Sacramento State University English Department when I got admitted into the English program, and last, but not least, Joe and Gay Haldeman, my wonderful and most supportive friends, who brought us to America. Haldeman is the winner of both the Nebula and Hugo Awards for his science fiction novels.

Special acknowledgments to the following Medium publications, where many of these poems and short forms have been published: *The Daily Cuppa, The Brain is a Noodle, Illumination, Literary Impulse, Know Thyself,*

Heal Thyself, *Being Known*, *The Lark*, *Poetry's Home*, *House of Haiku*, *Be Open*, and *Blue Insights*.

About the Author

Born and raised in Romania, Carmen Micsa moved to America in 1995, where she and her future husband Catalin Micsa have made Sacramento their home. Carmen Micsa has earned BA and MA degrees in English (Creative Writing) both from Sacramento State University. She has published her first book *Change Your Grip on Life Through Tennis* in 2016. She also published articles in a few local and national publications and a memoir piece *Grandpa's Garden* in the anthology *From Sac Home Myths & Other Untruths* together with some of her graduate school classmates.

In 2020, Micsa published her first poetry book *The PR – The Poetics of Running, A Book of Poetry in Motion*. It was her pandemic project that kept her sane and motivated to write and publish.

Besides writing, Micsa enjoys being a mother to her two beautiful and kind children Alex and

Sophia. She is also the broker/CEO/founder of her real estate company, Dynamic Real Estate, Inc., and prides herself for being organized and efficient in leading a balanced life.

Micsa is an avid runner, who has completed 14 marathons, including London, Boston, New York City, and Chicago. Besides running, Carmen loves to play tennis, swim, bike, and practice Pilates.

For more info on her books, please visit Carmen Micsa's website at www.carmenmicsabooks.com and her blog www.runningforrealestate.com.

www.ingramcontent.com/pod-product-compliance
Lightning Source LLC
Chambersburg PA
CBHW070424010526
44118CB00014B/1886